AF481890

ISBN: 978-628-01-5664-4

Editors: Balthazar Maille and Juliana Lopez Marulanda
Translation/Revision by Gladez Shorland Services Linguistiques
http://gs-serviceslinguistiques.com/

Illustrations by: AI (Midjourney & Canva)
Wildlife sounds: Juliana López Marulanda
Wildlife sounds edition: Julián Henao
Pollution sounds: PHySIC (Fundación Macuáticos Colombia)

THE JOURNEY OF ECO, THE CURIOUS DOLPHIN

To the children of the world...

On some pages of this book, just below the title, you will find a QR code like this one. Hold a smartphone camera over the QR code to listen to some ocean sounds recorded by the author.

1. A Day in the Ocean

Eco was happily swimming alongside his mother, enjoying the warmth of the sun and the gentle sway of the waves. "Mom, what are those sounds that I always hear underwater?" asked Eco curiously. His mother smiled and said, "Those are the songs of whales, the clicks of dolphins, and many other sounds we sea creatures use to communicate. Did you know female dolphins, like your grandma, are very special? They take care of our young and teach us many important things. That's why it's a wonderful idea for you to visit your grandma. She knows everything about ocean sounds and can tell you many stories."

2. Visiting Grandma

Eco headed towards the cave where his grandma lived. She was a wise dolphin with many stories to tell. "Grandma, I want to learn more about the sounds that I can hear underwater." said Eco excitedly. His grandma replied, "Of course, Eco. The ocean is full of fascinating sounds. Every creature has its own way of communicating. Today, I'll introduce you to some of them."

3.Dolphins and Their Signature Whistles

Eco was swimming near a group of young dolphins. "Hello, Eco." said one of them, with a distinctive whistle. "How do you know my name?" asked Eco. "We dolphins have our own signature whistles that act like names. Each of us has a unique whistle that helps others to identify us." explained the young dolphin. Eco's grandma added, "That's why they are called signature whistles. Try repeating your own whistle, and others will know where you are and be able to find you." Eco practiced his own signature whistle, feeling more connected to his family and friends. "It's amazing how we can stay together and coordinate just by using our whistles", thought Eco as he swam happily along.

4. The Singing Whales

Eco's grandma took him to a spot where humpback whales were swimming majestically. "Listen carefully, Eco!" said his grandma. Eco was amazed as he heard the long, melodic song of a humpback whale. "Why do you sing so loudly?" asked Eco, intrigued. The whale smiled and replied, "Our songs can last for more than 20 hours and travel thousands of kilometers underwater. This is how we stay in touch with our families, no matter the distance."

5. The Chomping Shrimp

Later, Eco and his grandma came across a colony of shrimp on the ocean floor. "Look at those shrimp, Eco!" said his grandma. "Did you know they make noise when they eat? Want to listen?" Eco nodded excitedly. Eco's grandma explained, "When shrimp feed, they make little crackling sounds as they move their pincers and bodies against the seafloor." Eco moved closer and listened carefully to the soft clicks. "Wow! I can hear them eating!" he exclaimed. Grandma smiled and added, "Yes, it's fascinating how they make sounds just by eating."

6. The Sperm Whale and the Echolocation

As they traveled through deeper waters, Eco and his grandma encountered a sperm whale. "Hello, little dolphin." said the sperm whale. "I'm using echolocation to navigate and hunt." "Echolocation? What's that?" asked Eco. "I emit clicks that bounce off objects. It's like seeing with your ears." explained the sperm whale. Eco tried making clicks and after several attempts, he managed to orient himself. "I did it, grandma! I can navigate with clicks!" "Well done, Eco!" said his grandma, proud of his progress.

7. The Confusing Noise

Eco and his grandma swam through an area with many boats. Suddenly, the noise was so loud that Eco got disoriented and lost sight of his grandma. "Grandma? Where is everyone?" he shouted, scared. Remembering what he had learned from the sperm whale, Eco made clicks to orient himself. His clicks bounced off nearby rocks, but he still couldn't find his family. Then, he used the signature whistle his grandma had taught him. He heard his mother's response in the distance. "I did it! I can find them now!" Eco exclaimed, swimming towards his family. His grandma smiled, pleased with what Eco had learned.

8. The Return Home

Eco and his mother were reunited thanks to the sound he had learned to use. "I'm so proud of you, Eco." said his mother. "You are now a young leader, ready to teach other dolphins what you've learned."

9.Additional Information and Activities

Dolphins and Signature Whistles

Individualized Communication: Dolphins use signature whistles to identify themselves and call one another, these whistles function like a unique name.

Meeting and Coordination: Signature whistles allow dolphins to find each other and coordinate in the vast ocean, helping to maintain group cohesion and organize their activities.

Humpback Whales

Social Behavior: Male whales use their song to communicate with other whales, especially during mating season.

Long Songs: Male humpback whales are known for their long and complex songs that can last more than 20 hours. These sounds can travel great distances underwater.

Snapping Shrimp

Sounds while Feeding: Shrimp produce sounds when they feed by moving their pincers and bodies along the ocean floor.

Sperm Whales and Echolocation

Seeing with their ears: Sperm whales feed in the deep ocean and use echolocation to see in the dark. They emit clicks that bounce off objects, allowing them to navigate and find food, such as giant squid. They can dive up to 2,800 meters underwater and they also use their clicks to communicate with each other.

Acoustic Pollution

Noise Pollution: Also known as acoustic pollution, this refers to the excessive noise generated by ships, sonar, and other human activities in the ocean. This noise affects marine animals, such as whales and dolphins, by interfering with their ability to communicate, navigate, and hunt. Prolonged exposure can disorient them or disrupt their natural behaviors. To reduce this impact, it is essential to regulate the use of sonar and develop quieter technologies for navigation.

Small Sound Experiments
(to be done with the help of an adult).

Create a Homemade Hydrophone:

Materials: A microphone, a sealable plastic bag, and waterproof tape.

Instructions: Place the microphone inside the plastic bag and seal it tightly with waterproof tape. Submerge the bag in a container of water, a pond, or a pool, and connect the microphone to a recording device. Try recording the sounds underwater and compare them with the sounds in the air.

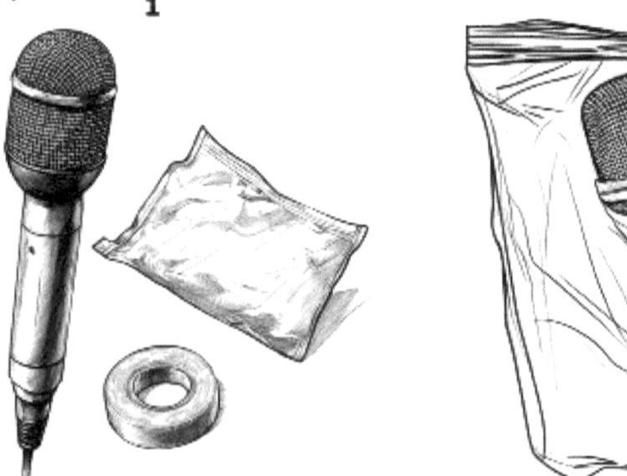

Create a Signature Whistle:

Materials: A voice recorder or a phone with a recording app.

Instructions: Each child creates their own signature whistle, records it, and practices. This whistle can then be used to play by calling each other from different parts of the house or garden, simulating how dolphins find each other in the ocean.

Voces del Mar Editorial is a publishing house dedicated to publishing books that promote environmental awareness and respect for marine biodiversity.